Lace

POEMS BY
Susan Wicks

ARTWORK BY
Elizabeth Clayman

Afterword by Philip Gross

First published in 2015
by Stonewood Press
97 Benefield Road, Oundle PE8 4EU
Tel: 0845 456 4838
books@stonewoodpress.co.uk
www.stonewoodpress.co.uk

All rights reserved
Poem © Susan Wicks, 2015
Artwork © Elizabeth Clayman, 2015
Afterword © Philip Gross, 2015
The authors and artist assert their moral rights to be
identified as the originators of this work

ISBN: 978-1-910413-10-4 (Paperback)
ISBN: 978-1-910413-11-1 (Hardback)

Distributed by Central Books
99 Wallis Road, London E9 5LN
Email: orders@centralbooks.com
Tel: 0845 458 9911

Printed and bound in the UK by Berforts Ltd., Hastings

Designed and typeset in Sabon 11pt/15pt
by www.silbercow.co.uk

Acknowledgments

Thanks are due to Ellen Montelius for her part in initiating the *Re-Collections* project. Thanks to Jo Wilcher, Abbi Bradford and Katrina Burton at the Tunbridge Wells Museum who saw the *Re-Collections* exhibition through to fruition.

The first poem in the sequence has been translated into French and published in both languages in the French magazine *La Traductière*.

Preface

Lace is the result of a collaboration between poet Susan Wicks and artist Elizabeth Clayman, and was created in 2010–11 as part of a commissioned project called *Re:Collections* when Tunbridge Wells Museum and Art Gallery opened their 'hidden' collections to a group of women writers and visual artists.

The 13 images in *Lace* are from a series of 50 charcoal drawings on gessoed wood panels. They are a response to a collection of antique lace housed within the 'hidden' collections in the Museum store-rooms. Though of varying quality, condition and origin, the lace remnants were each carefully interleaved between sheets of acid-free tissue. The random way the lace had deteriorated, been cut or torn, as well as the intricacy and variety of patterns, invited different responses: the journey of the lace, where it came from, who made it, who wore it, as well as the imaginings prompted by the actual threaded designs. Carefully drawing with soft vine charcoal which is fugitive, like dust, onto something of substance mirrored the labor-intensive act of lace-making itself, which constructs something fragile and delicate, yet often surprisingly robust.

The poems' meditation is at first largely abstract: an imaginative journey directly provoked by the frayed shapes and often defective patterns of the lace itself, as translated to the page by Elizabeth's drawings. But immediately a 'she' surfaces – at times the imagined maker(s) of the original fabric, at times the artist, and at times simply a woman looking out at a strange world through the complex grey curtain the lace provides. As the poem develops, it invites a reading as a study of, and eventual escape from, depression – but also as a study of the creative process itself, and the restraints female creators, particularly, have traditionally suffered from and overcome.

Elizabeth Clayman and Susan Wicks
June 2015

Lace

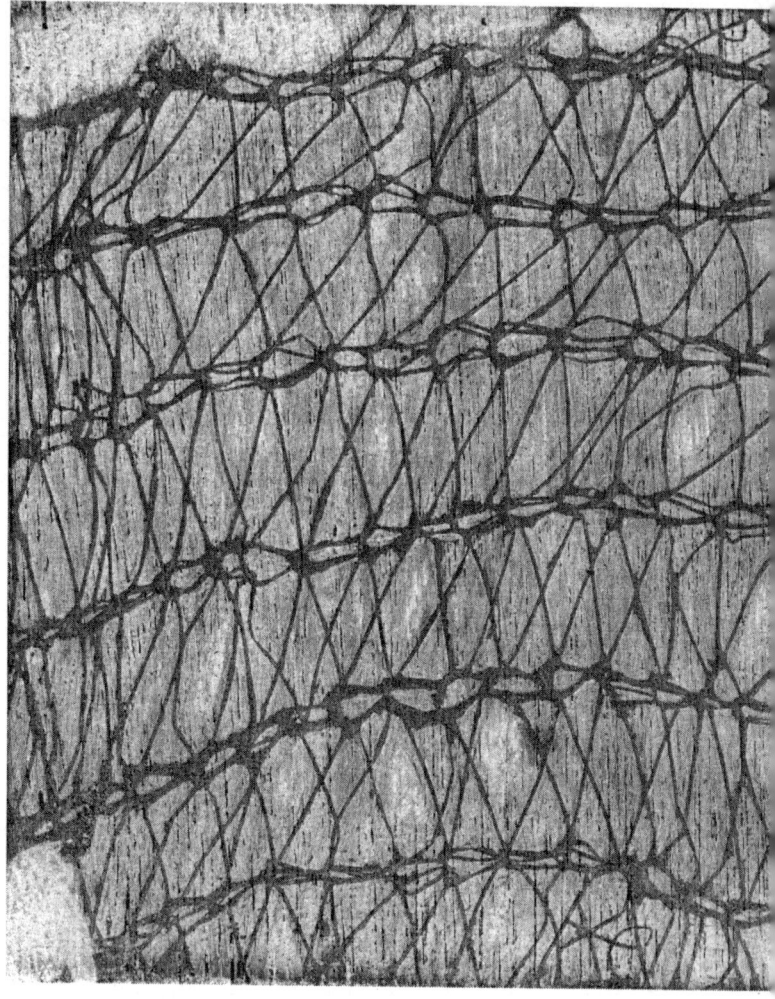

1

She has knitted her life up on needles
in thin thread, row upon row of stitches
pulled out of shape where an unseen something
has passed through – a pressing thumb,
a breath, a ball of fluff, a swarm
of buzzing wishes. Though she stretches and stretches
it will never be enough.

This lace she's knitted up
is strained and snagged, full of pulled stitches,
a soft hive of spaces
where the paler grey of morning
trickles in. All she can do now is go on –
take up her two grey needles,
listen to their clicking conversation
one against the other, mending this dark tatter,
knitting it better.

2

This is the turncoat of the mind:
she puts it on
and she is yes-or-no, and either/or,
she's duck-or-rabbit, Grecian vase/
two faces in profile about to speak or kiss.

She's a cave of stalactites
lengthening in shadow like pale teeth
or the tips of fingers/ she's the space between
encroaching pools of milk.
She's a Petri dish of multiplying cells/
the eye that sees them
bend and straighten
in a microscopic smile.

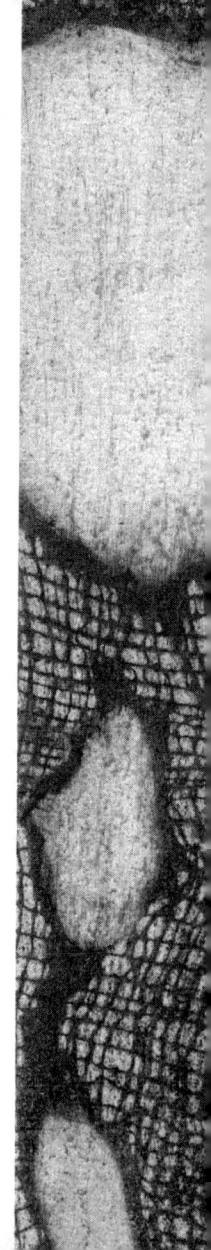

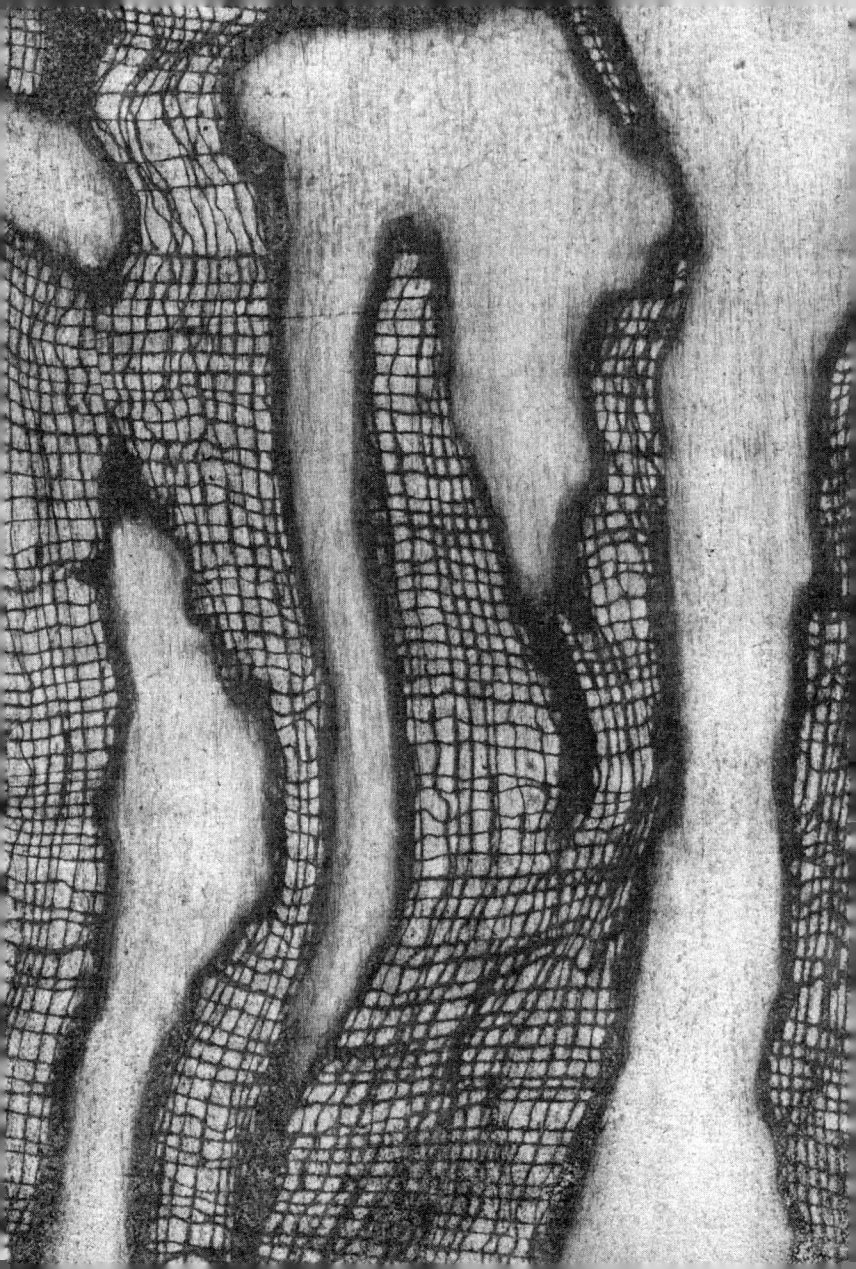

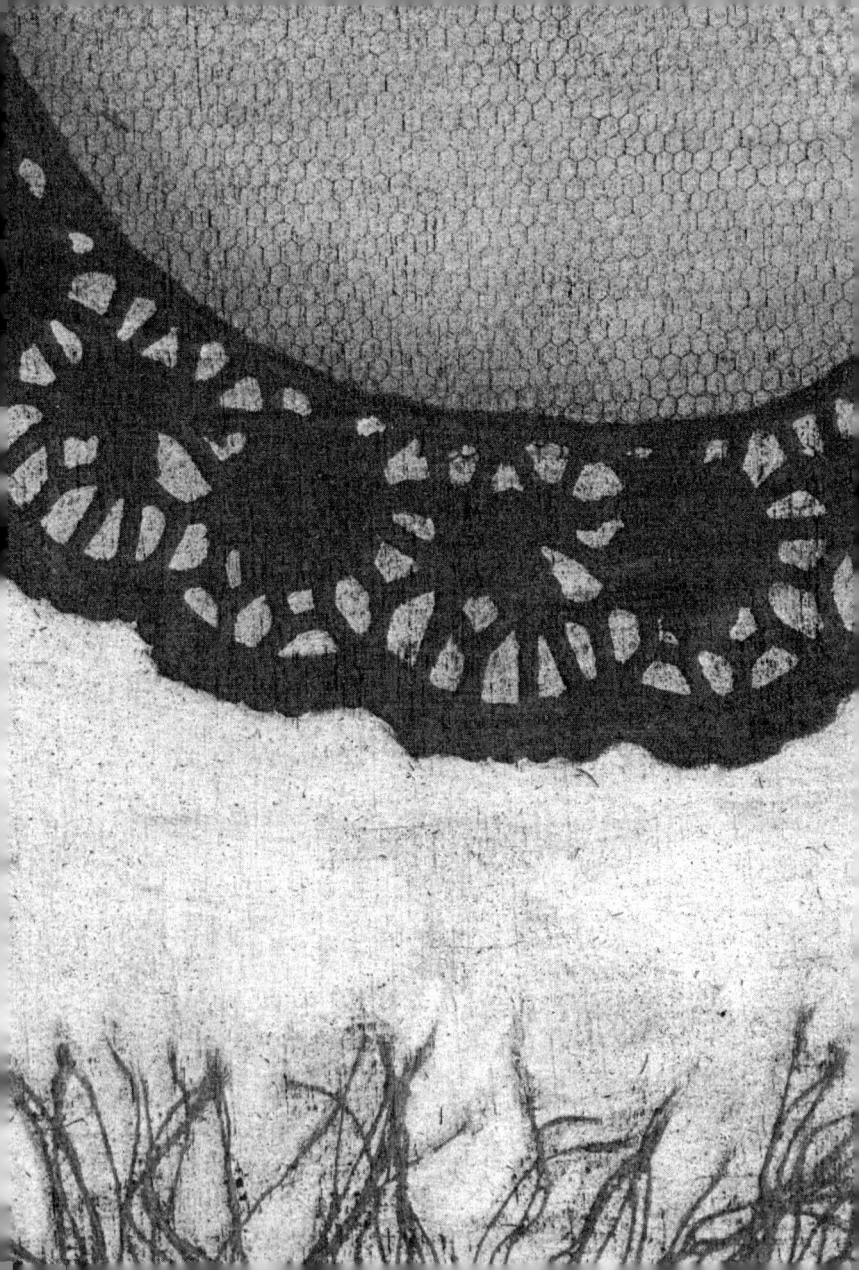

3

With a circle of dark lace
at her neck, her skin is matt,
veiled with a fine grey net

like fruit, as if high overhead
a flock of charcoal feathers
massed at her eyes' corners.

Do scarecrows come in grey
and dressed to kill
in lace, with a posy of grey roses?

It takes a kind of faith
or stubbornness to stand in this ripe grey
field with her arms outstretched.

The knuckles of her hands
are nowhere, yet they clench.
Under her unseen breasts

a fringe of threads
is wild as tangled grass
or hope, or flames, or fingers.

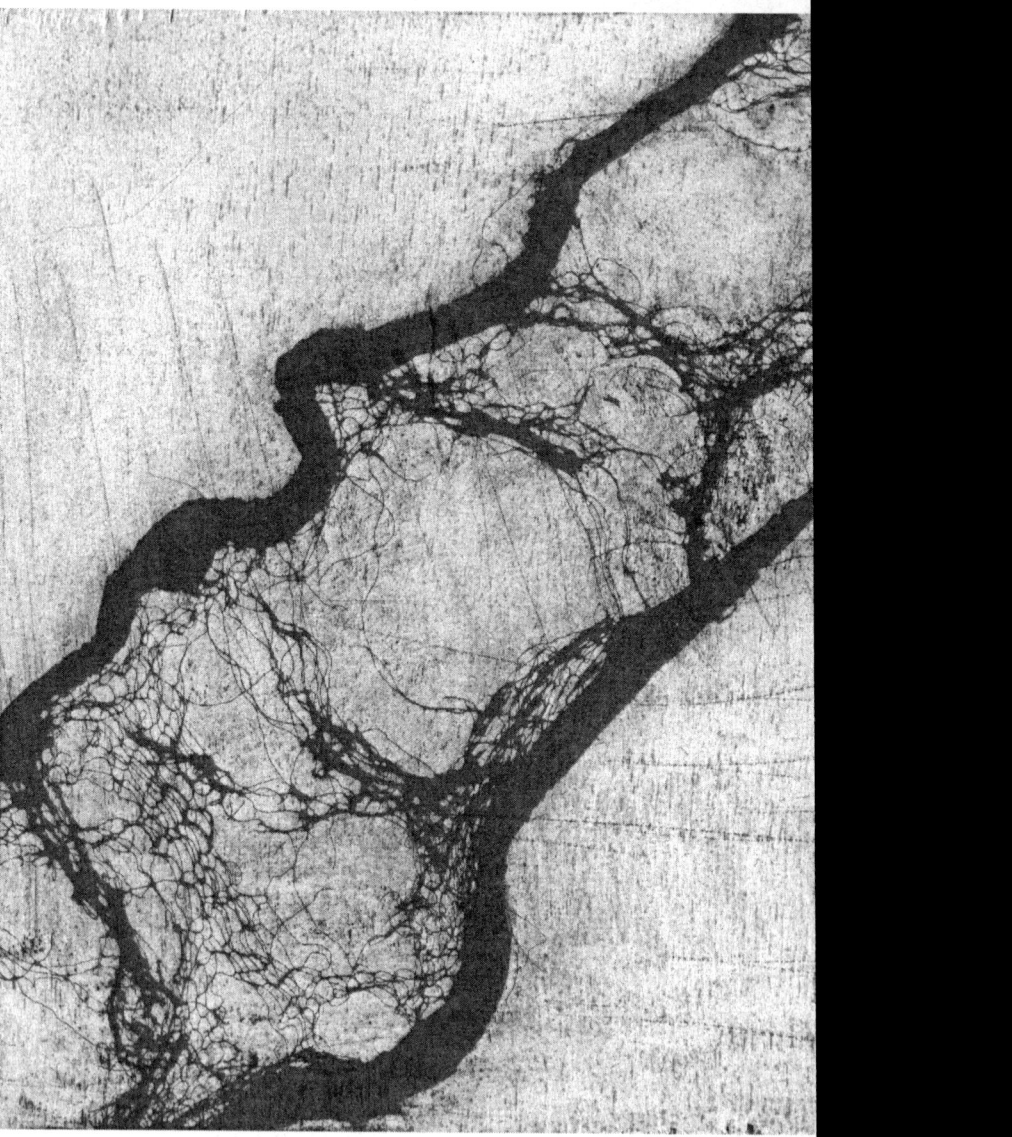

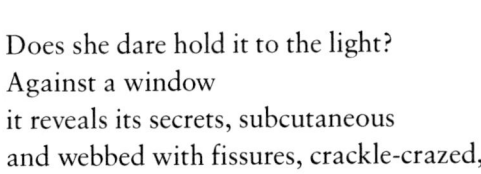

4

Does she dare hold it to the light?
Against a window
it reveals its secrets, subcutaneous
and webbed with fissures, crackle-crazed,
carious as an old tooth.

And what price truth?
Oh, let my body go. Let there
be numbness, paralysis.
The pain flows upwards, spreads its capillaries
as delicate as cobwebs, grey as antique lace
inside the bone.

And she's alone,
invisible, her future mapped
and veined like marble, foreign continent
criss-crossed by streams. She strokes the line
of ingress, as an explorer might.

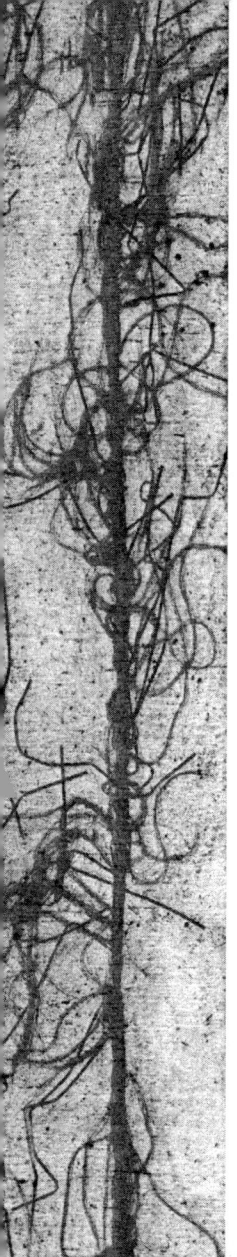

5

In moonlight, between pale birches
someone stands waiting, watches.
Somewhere among these trees
there's surely a trunk that's hollow,
where a child might hide? In a cloud
of her own white breath
she'll wait for years
till a crackling path
opens under the stars.

6

Here is a woman's body, turning white,
fattening like a slug. Each month it bleeds
a juice like sap, its head is full of light.
It cuts itself and what flows out is milk.

Inside, darkness quietly makes room
Until she's pale and empty – a cavity for heart
and one for stomach, fraying bag of womb
that moves its lips and lines itself with fur.

The dark flows downwards. No one sees it leave
and wind away, congeal to a dry skein,
the skein of who she was. Is it even grief?
Each snag's an unfelt love, an unlived life.

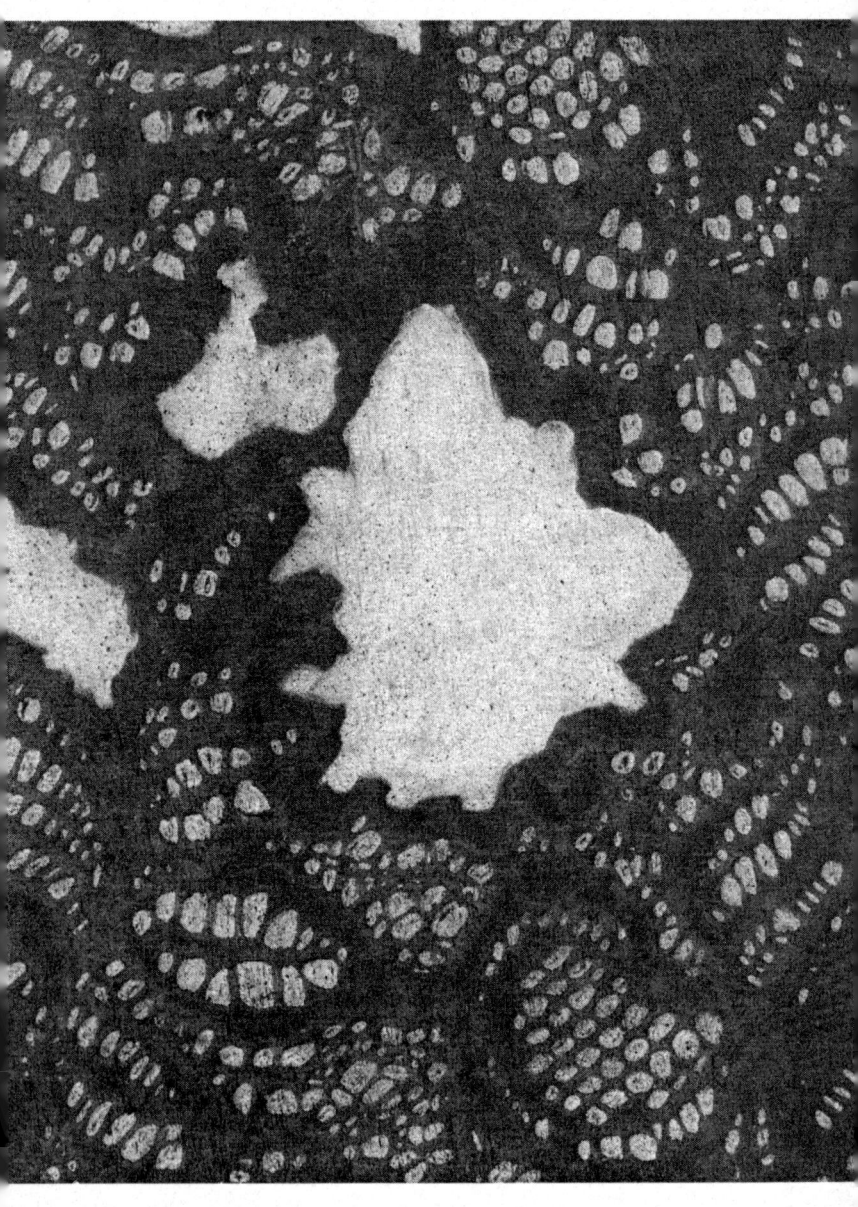

7

All morning she has been thinking of black flames,
the shapes of babies' feet or leaves, or pods of peas
nestled along a charcoal velvet spine,
a honeycomb of cells where blackened bees
bumble in and out in a reek of scorched wings.

But here at the centre is a torn space
where she can stand and breathe,
beautiful and empty as a lake
between black mountains. She can be here
at the farthest inlet of a creek
or here in the crescent of a volcanic beach –
or here, far out, where land's a distant pile of ash
and she can dive into hissing water
and resurface, plant her body upright like a flag.

8

Each day now she has given birth
to one of these – so many skeleton leaves
floating on water, nudging one another
this way or that – so many small conjectures
written in black lace. They never touch.
They move across the pale sky of the water
like small black moons
of honesty, their seeds long sprung,
their brittle envelopes long crumpled into earth.

So pick them out and shake them, put them in a bag
and hear them scratch and mew against the cloth.
Then lean and hold them under
while the ripples spread and settle, till the bubbles stop.

9

She's starting to understand
how something thin, laid flat,
can hold the dark. Her hand

fondles the glass's stem
as she watches a fire of vine-twigs
and the wine inside trembles.

The dark's been netted, safe:
this night that's gathered in
is a woman's life.

Outside, something has been erased,
has leaked away, or lifted
like a swarm of flies.

Here where the fine threads meet
night pools and bleeds
so steadily you hardly see it

like oil to a floating boom.
The sea reflects light,
its dark sequestered in a closed room.

10

She escapes it in her dreams
to a teeming forest where the leaves
leap upwards like green flames
from a heap of – what? Can they be seeds
or the shells of clambering turtles, human teeth
clacking a dialogue that's long-forgotten?

Charcoal butterflies
open their jewelled wings. If she can just stay asleep
she'll see a whole forest burn,
cool herself at its embers,
press her throbbing head against green.

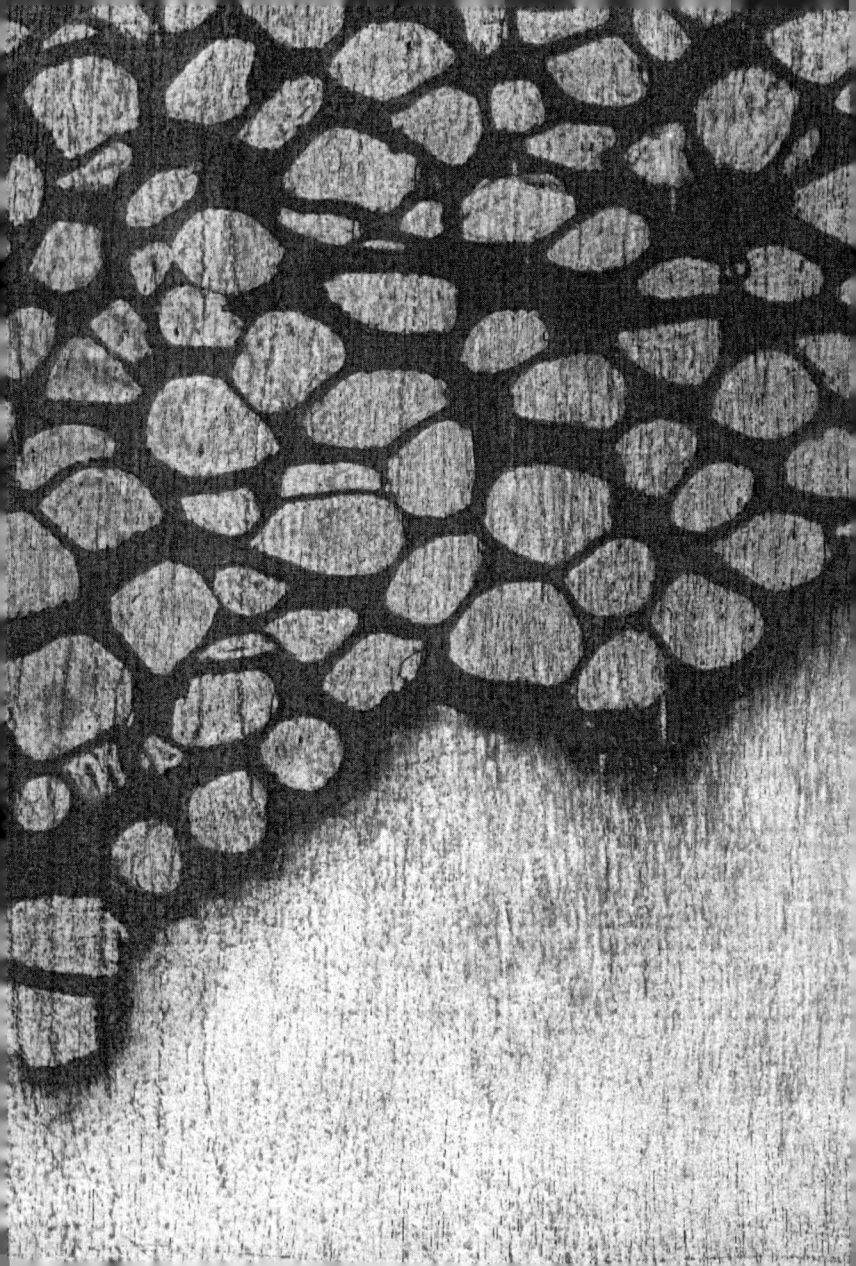

11

It's almost light:
her curtain made of holes
lifts on early morning:
stars of tangled dark
where drops of moisture
hang like breath on film
and fuse, bathing the glass.

Dawn. The hydrangeas blush.
Trees toss their leaves.
A crowd of little asters
blaze sudden yellow
and sway, and wave.

12

Is there something here
that never could escape? Each tiny knot
is neat as a Girl Guide's lanyard.
When she was twelve
she'd squeeze her eyes tight shut
and tie them in her sleep
behind her back
as if with a blindfold, time
and time again
till she was good enough.

Yet now beyond the net
the reefs and grannies blur
to a smudge of charcoal,
slide like antique silk
and disappear – outside
there's only air
and she is breathing it.

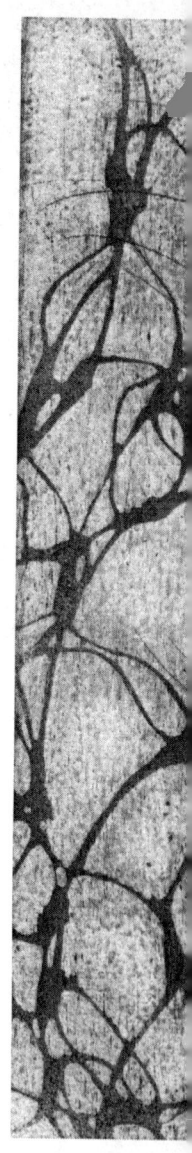

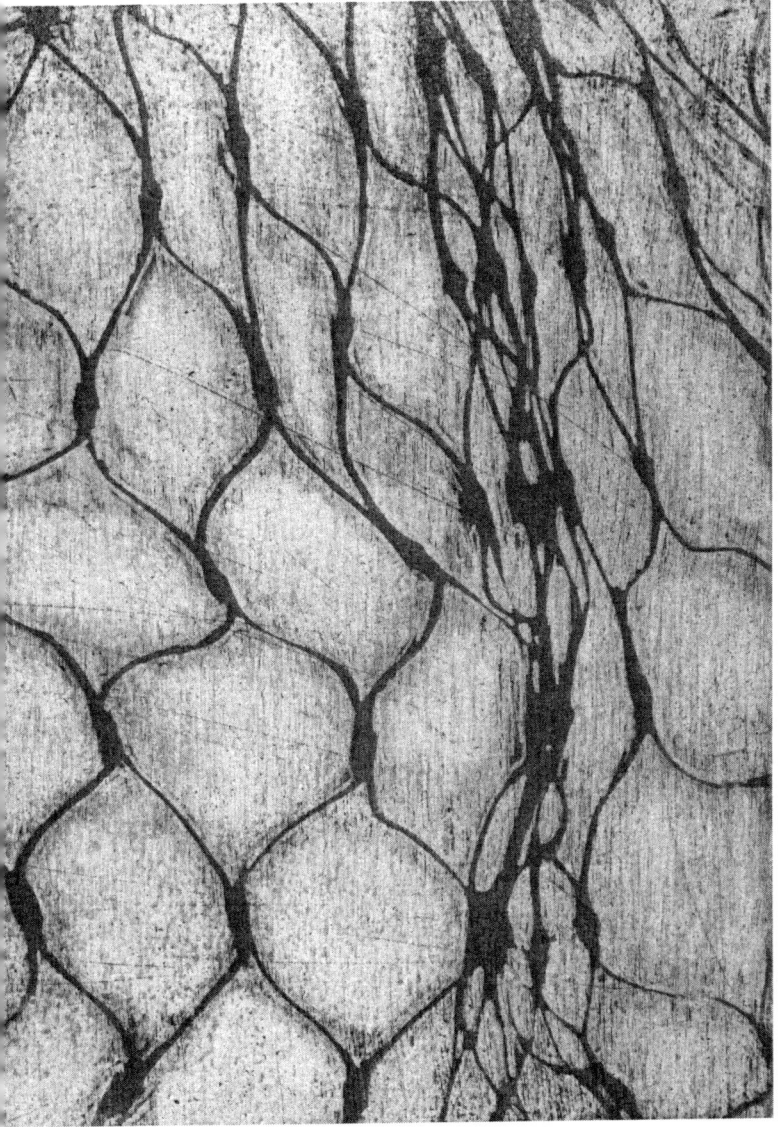

13

Who would have guessed this lace
would leave the hook and spread itself like waves
on sand and that the sand
would hold the water
trapped and shining, salted in its grain?

Low tide, and time
is inching shorewards, crawling, curling its white fingers,
fails,
and fizzes back
and crawls again, and breaks
man-high, slow-motion on the rocks, and glitters.

Afterword

Lacemaking: a by-word for intricate, painstaking work... It is hard to look, especially close up, without imagining the eye strain. But this is a craft full of paradox: it could be luxurious, the stuff of conspicuous display, or the decent trim around the edges of an ordinary life; it could be ornament or, equally, concealment; its net-like weave could suggest a safety net of domesticity, or a snare. We are grateful to museums that remnants, fragments, have been preserved, but there's a sadness, too, seeing these hints of lives and labour stopped in time.

Lace-making was women's work. In a differently gendered culture, it might have been an art form highly valued and preserved. As it is, the material is poignant for its being used and worn out, nearly lost... and anonymous, too. Thanks to the careful regard of Elizabeth Clayman and Susan Wicks, these 'stitches / pulled out of shape where an unseen something / has passed through' become eloquent.

There is a good deal more to this than pathos. At its heart, the craft of lacemaking is the applied skill of shaping spaces. The threads are the least of it. Rather, the knotting and the interweaving of them makes the pattern, with its delicacy and variety... and also its strength. In this art, the proportion of skill (the hours, the almost microscopic detail) to the substance (tiny fractions of ounces per thread) is very high indeed. And when the spaces are partly the product of decay or accident, then the possible readings of them grow and grow – again, in inverse proportion to the bulk of stuff. It is the absences that feed the poetry, as Susan Wicks gathers in the range of thirteen poems that, far from summing up a single narrative, suggest a widening range of lives that could be figured in these single glimpses.

Those glimpses, caught by the artist's eye, are openings. Elizabeth Clayman's images are made of vine charcoal, a soft, you could say tender, medium. Many of them preserve the sense of being seen through a slightly darkened film, like the preservative papers in a book of Victorian prints. But they also home in, bringing us up as close to the detail of the work as the lacemaker herself might have held it. At the same time, she selects, framing a range of forms of every texture, dense or flimsy, some with striking symmetries, some almost organic. All border on the abstract, with just enough hints of something figurative for the poetry to pick up an association, which becomes a metaphor... which in turn hints at a person, at a history, a life.

'Yes or no, or either/or': early on, a poem entertains the thought that this rich ambiguity could be illusion, like the familiar optical trick of the candle-stick that with a blink becomes the space between two faces. But it is not a trick. The thirteen poems here enact another message: that from these simple materials we are free to imagine, or to recognise, a wide range of experience, from playfulness to anxiety, from frustration to depression, to the vision of 'a torn space / where she can stand and breathe, / beautiful and empty as a lake / between black mountains'.

Another poem picks up the texture of sacking, up against the lace, and spins into the not-quite-comical picture of a scarecrow 'dressed to kill'... at the same time grim and poignant, and finally grand, as the scarecrow becomes partly wicker woman, partly corn goddess. Elsewhere the abstract forms suggest birch trunks, or maps, or the dry pods of honesty, medical images, a tideline – even turtles. This multiplicity is both playful and also, seriously, the point. For the original makers, this lace might have figured 'something here / that never could escape', but there *is* a liberation: '...now beyond the net 'the reefs and grannies blur / to a smudge of charcoal, / slide like antique silk 'and disappear – outside, there's only air / and she is breathing it.'

Together, the words and images here are a celebration of a fine aesthetic principle: that a tight, even exhaustive focus on the small thing, the simplest of stimuli, is not restriction but a liberation into a vast range of associations. It is a principle that especially opens out into collaboration. That collaboration might be between the artist and the viewer or, as here, between the artist and the poet. Susan Wicks is just one reader, one with the confidence and subtlety of a hugely accomplished writer, but her agile and heartfelt variations on these images empower every other reader/viewer of these images, and of the poems themselves. There is all this, the poetry says, and much more. Those spaces-between have a life of their own. The collaboration goes on, even beyond the lovely, balanced object of this little book. Any number of people will read and re-read, finding themselves and the lives of women throughout history... and yes, a man is writing this afterword, feeling that excitement. Like the best collaborations, this is not exclusive; we are all invited in.

Philip Gross
July 2015

ELIZABETH CLAYMAN grew up in South Carolina in the foothills of the Blue Ridge Mountains spending her summers on Cape Cod. She has a BA in English from Mount Holyoke College and University College London, and an MA in Fine Art from the University of Pennsylvania. She worked in Archaeological museums in the US and the UK drawing artifacts for academic publications. She works in a variety of mediums and is influenced by natural forms, cellular structures, fragmentation and patterns. Her work has been exhibited in both the UK and US and has also been used in EU research publications.

SUSAN WICKS has published six collections of poetry, three novels, a book of short stories and a short experimental memoir, *Driving My Father* (Faber, 1995). Her first collection of poems, *Singing Underwater* (Faber, 1992) won the Aldeburgh Poetry Festival Prize. Her third, *The Clever Daughter*, was a PBS Choice and shortlisted for both Forward and TS Eliot Prizes. Five of her books have received awards from the Poetry Book Society. She is also a multiple-award-winning translator of the French poet, Valérie Rouzeau. A new full collection of her own, *The Months*, is due from Bloodaxe in 2016.

Other Stonewood Press titles:

The Night Library poems by Anna Robinson
with artwork by Martin Parker

Dad's slideshow by Di Slaney

Hoad and other stories by Sarah Passingham

Small Grass poems by Jacqueline Gabbitas
with artwork by Frances Barry

Earthworks by Jacqueline Gabbitas

Notebook in hand: New and Selected Poems by John Rety

Said and done: New Writing from Brittle Star edited
Louisa Hooper, Jacqueline Gabbitas, David Floyd and
Martin Parker, with a foreword by Maureen Duffy

www.stonewoodpress.co.uk